DISCOVER
Oil Spills

by Barbara Brannon

Table of Contents

Introduction 2

Chapter 1 How Do People Use Oil? 4

Chapter 2 How Do Oil Spills Happen? 8

Chapter 3 What Happens After
an Oil Spill? 12

Conclusion 18

Concept Map 20

Glossary 22

Index 24

Introduction

People use **oil**. People use oil to live.

▲ Cars use oil.

Words to Know

containers

oil

oil spills

people

pipelines

plants

See the Glossary on page 22.

3

How Do People Use Oil?

People use oil in cars.

▲ Cars use oil.

People use oil in airplanes.

▲ Airplanes use oil.

People use oil in homes.

▲ Some furnaces use oil.

People use oil in offices.

▲ Some furnaces use oil.

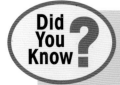
Did You Know?

Many people use furnaces. Furnaces heat homes. Furnaces heat offices.

People use oil in clothing.

▲ People use oil to make clothing.

People use oil in detergent.

▲ People use oil to make detergent.

People use oil in paint.

▲ People use oil to make paint.

People use oil in plastic.

▲ People use oil to make plastic.

People use oil in toothpaste.

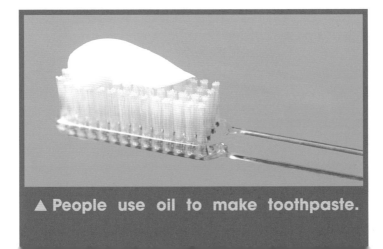

▲ People use oil to make toothpaste.

How Do Oil Spills Happen?

Ships have **oil spills**.

▲ This ship had an oil spill.

Trucks have oil spills.

▲ This truck had an oil spill.

Containers have oil spills.

Pipelines have oil spills.

▲ This pipeline had an oil spill.

Chapter 3

What Happens After an Oil Spill?

Oil spills hurt birds.

▲ Oil spills can kill birds.

Oil spills hurt whales.

▲ Oil spills can kill whales.

Oil spills hurt seals.

▲ Oil spills can kill seals.

Oil spills hurt fish.

▲ **Oil spills can kill fish.**

Oil spills hurt **plants**.

▲ Oil spills can kill plants.

Oil spills hurt the land.

Conclusion

Oil spills hurt Earth.

▲ Oil spills can harm plants, animals, and the environment.

Concept Map

Oil Spills

How Do People Use Oil?	How Do Oil Spills Happen?	What Happens After an Oil Spill?
cars	ships	birds hurt
airplanes	trucks	whales hurt
homes	containers	seals hurt
offices	pipelines	fish hurt
clothing		plants hurt
detergent		land hurt
paint		
plastic		
toothpaste		

Glossary

containers objects that hold matter

Containers have oil spills.

oil a natural resource

People use oil in cars.

oil spills oil that gets on land or in water

Oil spills hurt Earth.

people human beings

People use oil to heat offices.

pipelines pipes used to move oil

Pipelines have oil spills.

plants living things that can not move around

*Oil spills hurt **plants**.*

Index

airplanes, 4, 20

birds, 12, 20

cars, 2, 4, 20

Earth, 18

fish, 15, 20

homes, 5, 20

land, 17, 20

offices, 5, 20

oil, 2, 4–7, 20

oil spills, 8–10, 12, 14–18, 20

paint, 7, 20

people, 2, 4–7, 20

pipelines, 10, 20

plants, 16, 18, 20

plastic, 7, 20

seals, 14, 20

ships, 8, 20

toothpaste, 7, 20